9000785977

D1613697

EASY READING

A New True Book

SEABIRDS

By Alice K. Flanagan

Subject Consultant
David E. Willard, Ph.D.
Collection Manager of Birds at the Field Museum
of Natural History, Chicago, Illinois

Children's Press®
A Division of Grolier Publishing
New York   London   Hong Kong   Sydney
Danbury, Connecticut

A cape cormorant pair

For all those whose spirit soars near the sea

PHOTO CREDITS

Animals, Animals — © J & B Photo, 2; © Fritz Prenzel, 8; © Johnny Johnson, 9, 45; © Henry Ausloos, 10; © Doug Allan, 12 (left); © John Eastcott/Yva Momatiuk, 17 (left), 36 (left); © John Gerlach, 19; © Mark Chappell, 21; © Joe McDonald, 23; © Victoria McCormick, 25, 36 (right); © Patti Murray, 27 (left); © E. R. Degginger, 27 (top right); © G. L. Kooyman, 27 (bottom right); © Ray Richardson, 29 (right); © Alfred B. Thomas, 31 (left); © Lon. E. Lauber, 31 (right); © Peter Weimann, 39; © Michael Brooke, 42 (left); © Ben Osborne, 42 (bottom right)

Jeff Foott Productions — © Jeff Foott, 11 (right), 15, 29 (top), 33 (right), 34

Valan Photos — © Michel Julien, 4; © Dennis Schmidt, 7; © J. A. Wilkinson, 11 (left); © Aubrey Lang, cover, 12 (right), 33 (left); © Stephen J. Krasemann, 14; © Joyce Photographics, 17 (right), 42 (top right); © R. Berehin, 22; © Roy Luckow, 37; © Pam E. Hickman, 40

Vantage Art — map, 6

COVER: Colony of black-browed albatrosses on the Falkland Islands

Project Editor: Dana Rau
Electronic Composition: Biner Design
Photo Research: Flanagan Publishing Services

Library of Congress Cataloging-in-Publication Data

Flanagan, Alice.
    Seabirds / by Alice K. Flanagan.
        p. cm. — (A New true book)
    Includes index.
    Summary: An overview of seabirds around the world and the special adaptations they make to their marine environment.
    ISBN 0-516-01088-3
    1. Sea birds—Juvenile literature. [1. Sea birds. 2. Birds.] I. Title.
QL676.2.F62 1996
598.29'24—dc20   95-25804
                                       CIP AC

CONTENTS

Gannets nest on
Bonaventure Island in
Quebec, Canada. Most
nests are spaced only
beaks apart.

4

WORLD TRAVELERS

Thousands of screeching birds nest among jagged rocks of Bonaventure Island. For several months each year, this island is one the largest seabird refuges on earth.

During the rest of the year, seabirds roam throughout earth's water world. Almost three-fourths of the earth's surface is covered by water. Much of it is unexplored by humans. Yet, millions of birds explore it every year.

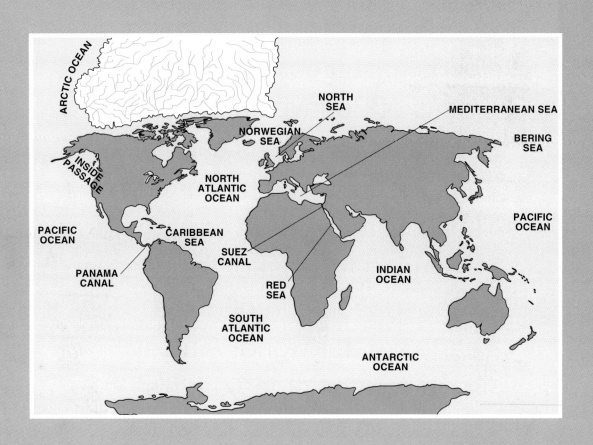

ARCTIC OCEAN

NORTH
SEA

MEDITERRANEAN SEA

NORWEGIAN
SEA

BERING
SEA

INSIDE
PASSAGE

NORTH
ATLANTIC
OCEAN

PACIFIC
OCEAN

PACIFIC
OCEAN

CARIBBEAN
SEA

SUEZ
CANAL

PANAMA
CANAL

INDIAN
OCEAN

RED
SEA

SOUTH
ATLANTIC
OCEAN

ANTARCTIC
OCEAN

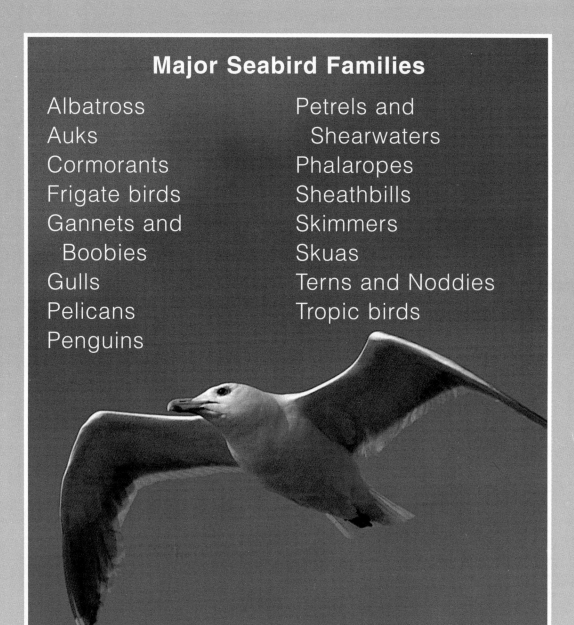

Major Seabird Families

Albatross	Petrels and
Auks	Shearwaters
Cormorants	Phalaropes
Frigate birds	Sheathbills
Gannets and	Skimmers
Boobies	Skuas
Gulls	Terns and Noddies
Pelicans	Tropic birds
Penguins	

An Australian pelican landing on water

WHAT'S SO SPECIAL ABOUT SEABIRDS?

Seabirds are well adapted to life at sea. Most seabirds have webbed feet to help them take off from and land on water. Cormorants use their webbed feet to propel themselves through water. Storm-petrels look like they are walking on water when they are taking off and landing.

Seabirds also have special wing shapes. Most seabirds, such as fulmars, albatross, and shearwaters, have long,

A black-browed albatross landing on a grassy knoll on the Falkland Islands

9

Razorbill auk

narrow wings for better flight.
Auks have short, narrow
ones. This helps them "fly"
underwater with great skill.
Penguins have even shorter
wings. They cannot fly in the
air at all, but they are
unbeatable underwater.

Seabird feathers are thick. Each day, seabirds must spend several hours taking care of their feathers, or preening them.

(Left) Seabirds have flexible necks, and most can turn them 380 degrees when preening their feathers.
(Right) Birds oil their feathers to make them waterproof and to keep body heat from escaping.

(Left) Seabirds drink seawater freely, and dispose of the harmful amounts of salt through openings in their beaks. (Right) Many seabirds remain paired for life. At breeding time, they raise their offspring together.

They use their beaks or the backs of their heads to take oil from a special gland above their tails. With this oil, they cover, or lubricate, their feathers to waterproof them.

SEABIRD
COLONIES

When breeding, seabirds
live together in large
communities, or colonies.
Usually the colonies are
located on islands, cliffs,
or sandbars where they
are safe from predators
and close to the sea where
food is abundant. The
descendants of some

13

Common murres do not build nests. They crowd together on ridges of cliffs.

colonies often remain at the same site for centuries.

There are many advantages to living in large colonies. Group living is generally safer than living alone. Members warn each

White pelicans feeding

other of danger. They are more successful at keeping predators away. They also find more food sources. A flock of pelicans, for example, can encircle and trap schools of fish that one pelican could not handle alone.

MIGRATION

After every breeding season, seabirds leave their nests to head for better feeding sites. Months later, they return to the same breeding grounds, often to the same nest. This event is called migration. It is repeated every year of a bird's life.

In cooler climates, birds fly to warmer areas,

(Left) Black skimmers on a Louisiana delta during their spring migration. (Above) A lone giant petrel feeding at sea.

sometimes even across the equator. At the end of an Antarctic summer, for example, some petrels head north into the western Atlantic to feed in the rich fishing waters off

North America. Other petrels spend the winter at sea, not far from land. They drift with the winds, until it is time to breed again.

Short-tailed shearwaters leave Australia and fly for five months. They journey north to Japan and then to the Bering Sea. Finally, they turn south along the west coast of North America and cross the open Pacific on their way back home to Australia.

Arctic terns become very attached to their territories and often return to the same area each year.

Arctic terns spend almost their entire lives in the air. After breeding at the Arctic Circle, they fly 11,000 miles (17,700 kilometers) south to the food-rich waters of Antarctica. When they arrive, it is just about time to begin their return trip.

FINDING THEIR WAY AT SEA

Seabirds are very skillful at finding their way in unmarked oceans. Yet, we are still uncertain as to how they know which routes to take. When a young bird leaves its nest, it spends a lot of time wandering to get familiar with the landmarks of its home. These landmarks will guide it

Fulmars spend most of their lives at sea. They return to land to breed.

during the final stage of the return trip of its migration.

Some birds learn the specific route from the elders of the group they fly with on the journey. But birds who fly alone must learn on their own.

The fall and early spring sky becomes a freeway of bird activity.

Along shorelines, seabirds use visual signs, such as cliffs and lighthouses, to guide them. Some may use sound waves (distant echoes from cliffs and mountains) and even smell. But what do they do when land is out of sight? And how do they travel at night?

Once away from land,
birds must learn to live on
the vast ocean, sometimes
for months at a time. There
is nowhere to rest but on
the rolling waves, or on an
occasional ship or piece of
driftwood floating by.
Violent storms, high winds,
towering waves, and

During their
migration,
some birds
rest on ships
at sea.

extremes in temperature bring danger at every turn.

Studies show that birds use the position of the sun to find their way when land is not visible. At night they take their direction from the stars. But what happens on cloudy nights, or in stormy weather, or when winds take birds off course? They seem to rely on an inborn sense of direction to reach their destination. Their inner clock and compass work

Sunset in the Hawaiian Islands

like a computer map
telling them where they
are and in what direction
they need to fly. As yet,
we do not know how this
amazing system works,
but we know it is there.

AMAZING FISHING FEATS

   Birds use a variety of fishing methods. Some fish by day and others by night. Some scoop up tiny plankton on the surface of the water. Others chase fish underwater. Some prefer to fly alongside ships and eat the waste thrown from them. A few even steal the catch of other birds.

(Above) Frigate birds and brown pelicans in Ecuador wait for castaways from a small fishing boat.
(Top right) A black skimmer picks up small fish on the surface of the water.
(Bottom right) An emperor penguin fishes in the seas of Antarctica.

Seabirds live almost totally on animal matter. They eat fish and tiny animals called zooplankton, or krill.

While albatross and shearwaters are still flying, or swimming on the surface, they pluck fish from the water. Brown pelicans, gannets, and boobies can "plunge-dive" from distances of 100 feet (30 meters) or more above the water. Red-necked phalaropes spin on the surface of the water to bring tasty plankton to the top. In acrobatic feats, frigate birds can catch flying fish

(Top) Brown pelicans fold their wings close to their bodies and enter the water like a bullet. (Right) A Wilson's phalarope tries to bring plankton to the top of the water.

in midair. Auks, penguins, and cormorants hunt superbly underwater.

SEABIRDS OF THE NORTH ATLANTIC TO THE CARIBBEAN SEA

If we take a trip by ship around the world, we see many kinds of seabirds. Leaving New York harbor in the northern Atlantic Ocean, our ship is followed by herring gulls. Once out of reach of land,

(Left) Gulls are scavengers. They eat any kind of food or garbage on sea and shore.
(Right) Black-legged kittiwakes winter at sea. When they return to their colonies, older birds arrive about a month before the younger ones.

black-legged kittiwakes and then gannets appear. By the time we reach Europe, fulmars and manx shearwaters fly overhead. We sight storm-petrels, too.

Sailing south and west into the Caribbean Sea brings us into a rich feeding area for wintering seabirds. Brown boobies are the most numerous in these waters. We also hear a few tropic birds whistling as they pass our ship. When we are on deck at night, we see them at the surface of the water feeding on squid. At harbors along the way, brown pelicans, frigate birds, and a variety of

(Left) Boobies come to land only to breed. Different species of bobbies are named for their colorful webbed feet— brown, red, and blue.
(Above) The red-billed tropic bird flies gracefully in the air. On the ground, it shuffles along on its breast, because it cannot stand.

gulls welcome us. We follow the graceful frigate birds into the Panama Canal on our way to the largest ocean of the world—the Pacific.

SEABIRDS OF THE VAST PACIFIC

While our ship slowly passes through the Panama Canal, we see flocks of gulls, brown pelicans, and cormorants.

A flock of brown pelicans flying along the coast of Mexico

Following the coast north to San Francisco, boobies, terns, black skimmers, shearwaters, and storm-petrels appear. They even come aboard at night.

From San Francisco we turn southwest and cross the northern Pacific where the albatross is abundant. Heading toward New Zealand, in the southern Pacific, there are flocks of black noddies and a variety of terns. Nearing the coast, we see diving

(Left) New Zealand has the greatest variety of seabirds in the world, including the pied shag.
(Right) A black noddy and its chick

petrels, pied shags, shearwaters, and gulls galore!

Next, we head for Australia, which is a popular wintering area for albatross, petrels, shearwaters, and black noddies. Here, too, are the famous little penguin colonies.

Continuing north to the ports of Japan, we find trained cormorants bringing in fish for Japanese fishermen.

A fisherman and his trained cormorant

SEABIRDS OF THE INDIAN OCEAN TO THE ARCTIC SEA

Our ship takes us southwest into the Indian Ocean, then north through the Red Sea and Suez Canal to the Mediterranean Sea. Here, there are few seabirds. But when we move onward to the North Sea, fulmars, gannets, and

White-tailed tropic birds fly over the Seychelles Islands in the Indian Ocean.

auks are in sight daily. Towering oil rigs are resting places for songbirds and birds of prey.

Through the Norwegian Sea, we sail north to the Arctic Circle. The region is packed with noisy, breeding terns. We pass the island of Rost, where Atlantic puffins breed. Ahead are many

Millions of puffins live in the Arctic waters of the Atlantic and Pacific oceans.

colonies of gannets, skuas, kittiwakes, and cormorants. As we journey north, we pass Bear Island, where thousands of Arctic dovekie nest. Finally, we are at Spitsbergen, one of the most spectacular colonies of breeding seabirds.

SEABIRDS OF THE SOUTH ATLANTIC

Our southern journey takes us back across the Panama Canal and into the southern Atlantic Ocean. We travel along northern Brazil where rich fishing grounds bring a lot of seabird activity, including Wilson's storm-petrels, sooty shearwaters, and greater shearwaters.

(Above) A yellow-nosed albatross and its chick (Above right) Young emperor penguins quickly learn how to survive on their own. (Bottom right) The northern giant petrel does not leave its eggs, even in bad weather.

We pass the Falkland Islands, where more than fifty species of birds breed. Soon, we enter the Antarctic Ocean, the richest area of plant plankton in the world. We see king penguins among flocks of albatross, petrels, and sheathbills.

The South Sandwich Islands are home to millions of chinstrap penguins. Farther out at sea, we watch playful Adélie penguins diving off large, drifting ice rafts. Finally, we come to the shores of Antarctica. This is home to colonies of fulmars and petrels and the only nesting habitat for the emperor penguin.

Our arrival in Antarctica brings our trip to a close. But our journey with seabirds is not over. We board an airplane for the trip home. This time we will see earth as seabirds do—from the sky.

Like most penguins in Antarctica, king penguins live in
huge colonies called rookeries.

GLOSSARY

abundant (uh-BUN-duhnt) — more than enough

adapt (a-DAPT) — to become suitable to function under certain conditions

breed (BREED) — to produce or increase by reproduction

canal (kuh-NAL) — an artificial waterway for boats

century (SEN-chuh-ree) — a period of one hundred years

colony (KAHL-uh-nee) — a group of living things of one kind living together

compass (KAHM-puhs) — a device that indicates direction on the earth's surface

descendant (dih-SEN-duhnt) — coming from a line of ancestors

destination (des-ti-NAY-shun) — the point at the end of a journey

dispose (dis-POHZ) — to get rid of

elder (EL-der) — one who is older

encircle (en-SER-kuhl) — to surround

equator (ee-KWAY-tuhr) — an imaginary circle around the earth, equally distant from the north and south poles

extreme (ek-STREEM) — to a very great degree

gland (GLAND) — an organ in the body that prepares a substance to be used by the body

habitat (HAB-i-tat) — the place where an animal lives in nature

inborn (IN-BAWRN) — natural ability that does not have to be learned

krill (KRIL) — tiny, floating sea creatures

lubricate (LOO-bri-kate) — to apply oil to

migration (my-GRAY-shun) — to move from one country, or place, to another at specific times

offspring (AWF-spring) — the young of an animal

plankton (PLANGK-ten) — tiny floating plants and animals in water

predator (PRED-at-ur) — an animal that kills and eats other animals

preen (PREEN) — to smooth with the bill

prey (PRAY) — an animal hunted or killed by another animal for food

propel (proh-PEL) — to push forward

refuge (REF-yooj) — a place that provides shelter or protection

sandbar (SAND-bar) — a ridge of sand formed in water by tides or currents

school (SKOOL) — a large number of one kind of fish swimming together

sound waves (SOWND WAYVZ) — waves that carry sound through the air

species (SPEE-sheez) — animals that form a distinct group made up of related individuals

waterproof (WAW-tuhr-proof) — not letting water through

webbed feet (WEBD FEET) — feet with toes joined by membranes

INDEX

(**Boldface** page numbers indicate illustrations.)

ABOUT THE AUTHOR

Alice K. Flanagan is a freelance writer and bird advocate. She considers her strong interest in birds, and a feeling of kinship with them, a symbol of her independence and freedom as a writer. She enjoys writing, especially for children. "The experience of writing," she says, "is like opening a door for a caged bird, knowing you are the bird flying gloriously away."

Ms. Flanagan lives with her husband in Chicago, Illinois, where they take great pleasure in watching their backyard birds.